How to Ruin Your Sister's LIFE

06 07 08 09 10 BID 10 9 8 7 6 5 4 3 2 1

ISBN-13: 978-0-7407-6072-3
ISBN-10: 0-7407-6072-6

Library of Congress Control Number: 2006923252

Illustrations copyright © 2006 by Adrienne Hartman

www.andrewsmcmeel.com

ATTENTION: SCHOOLS AND BUSINESSES
Andrews McMeel books are available at quantity discounts with bulk purchase for educational, business, or sales promotional use. For information, please write to: Special Sales Department, Andrews McMeel Publishing, LLC, 4520 Main Street, Kansas City, Missouri 64111.

How to
Ruin Your
Sister's LIFE

Mary McHugh

Illustrated by Adrienne Hartman

**Andrews McMeel
Publishing, LLC**

Kansas City

Sisters love each other, hate each other, torment each other, stick up for each other, and are experts at making each other miserable. Any woman with a sister will tell you hilarious stories about terrible things her sister did to her when she was little . . . and when she was dating . . . and when she was grown up with a family. Older sisters never seem to forgive their younger sisters for being born and ruining their star billing in the family, and younger sisters resent their big sisters for treating them as inferior beings. Forever after, they try to get even.

Here are some new, fresh ways to torment your sister, whether she's six or sixty:

When she's peeling from a bad sunburn,
tell her she has leprosy and her toes will fall off.

When her boyfriend comes over,
be sure to show him the adorable house you
made for your trolls out of her Kotex box.

Borrow her favorite
cashmere sweater and spill
soy sauce all over it.

Tell her that whenever
she has sex, there has to
be a doctor present.

Tell your younger sister that
your mother told you she loves
you best and wishes she had
never had another child.

Marry her boyfriend.

Tell her there's no Santa Claus, Easter bunny, or tooth fairy all on the same day.

Throw away the heads to all her Barbie dolls.

As you're leaving for a business trip to Paris, call her and tell her being a housewife is "really important, too."

If you have three beautiful, well-behaved children and a husband who adores you, tell your single sister you hope her career is as fulfilling as your life.

Take a picture of your fifty-five-year-old sister nude, brushing her teeth.

Tell her you were the only child your parents wanted. The others were all accidents.

When your little sister says, "You can't make me do that—you're not my mother!" say, "Oh, but I *am* your mother. I had you when I was only thirteen and my mother had to raise you."

Get your sister a date with a gay guy and tell her if anyone can convert him, she can.

Tell your thirteen-year-old sister's boyfriend that she still sucks her thumb at night.

Take your little sister to the corner and try to sell her for $1. Complain to your mother that nobody wanted to buy her.

Set her hair on fire "by mistake" and then cut it off in clumps to cover up the damage.

When you're picking out bridesmaids' dresses for your wedding, choose a color and style that makes your sister look ten years older.

Cut up her Christmas stocking and flush the pieces down the toilet.

Tell her she's adopted but your
parents don't want her to know it.

Say, "You'd better do what I say
or I won't be your friend."

Before she drifts off to sleep, whisper, "Mom and Dad had another daughter before you, but they had to trade her in because she was bad, so you'd better be good all the time."

Destroy her by saying,
"You sound exactly like Mom."

Take your little sister to the mall and lose her.
Tell your mother she went off to live with another
family and she looked very happy.

When your show-offy sister plays the piano
for relatives and friends, sneer and laugh loudly
whenever she makes a mistake.

She has a glamorous, exciting job in the city.
You're bartending until something better turns up.
Tell her you hope she can stand all that pressure.

Ask people if they don't think it's strange that your sister is the only blonde in a family of brunettes and hint that she must have had a different father.

When you're with your friends and your sister shows up, pretend you never saw her before in your life.

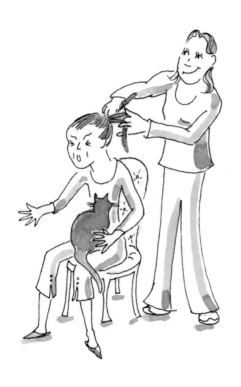

Braid your sister's hair so tightly she looks like she's just had a bad face-lift.

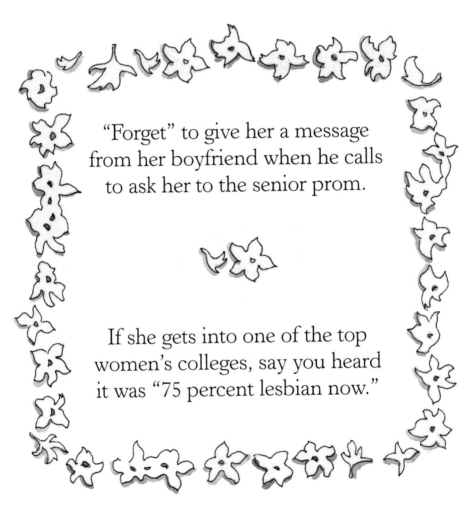

"Forget" to give her a message
from her boyfriend when he calls
to ask her to the senior prom.

If she gets into one of the top
women's colleges, say you heard
it was "75 percent lesbian now."

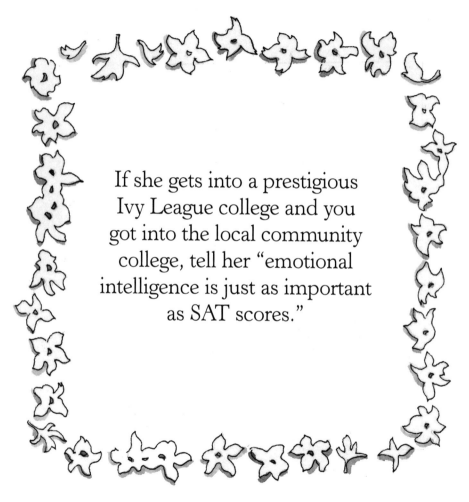

If she gets into a prestigious Ivy League college and you got into the local community college, tell her "emotional intelligence is just as important as SAT scores."

Men follow her around like puppy dogs.
You haven't had sex in a year. Ask her if she
has heard of the new trend—celibacy.

She majored in economics and employers
are begging her to join their Wall Street firms.
You majored in philosophy and are working as
an office temp. Say you hope she won't be bored
by the same routine all the time.

Tell your little sister you tried to wash her blankie and it got swallowed up by the bad washing machine.

Borrow your sister's new car and fill it up with diesel fuel. Say you didn't realize it would completely wreck the engine.

Your sister is president of her sorority.
You marched in the gay pride parade.
Wonder out loud if sororities are still "relevant"
in the twenty-first century.

Your sister's children are jocks.
Yours are intellectuals. Give her a copy of
Sports as a Religion in America.

If your sister is the "good one"
and you're the "bad one," enjoy it.

If your sister can eat everything and never
gain an ounce and you're always on a diet,
ask her if she's bulimic.

You're having a bad-hair day
and your sister looks like her usual
perfect self. Take her for a ride in
your convertible with the top down.

Tell your sister that lifting weights
will give her a fat neck.

Read her diary and quote from it the
next time she brings a date home—
especially if there's a really
good part about him.

If your sister asks you if you
know an exciting place to go for a
vacation, send her to New Jersey.

Offer to color your sister's hair and
use at least three colors.

When your sister needs "something borrowed"
on her wedding day, lend her your cold.

When the phone rings, say to your sister,
"That must be your real mother.
She said she'd call today."

If you are an identical twin, go out
with her boyfriend and pretend to be her
and tell him you have a fake leg.

The first time you take your
younger sister to the beach,
tell her that sharks like to eat
little girls, but they would only
take a small bite of her
because she tastes sour.

Rent *The Exorcist* and tell your
little sister she must be possessed
by the devil like Linda Blair
because she's so evil.

When *Invasion of the Body Snatchers*
is on TV, tell your little sister
it's true and she's next.

In the middle of your sister's divorce, tell her if she had lost twenty pounds she'd still be married.

Your sister wants to become an actress.
Tell her she should learn to type as a backup.

Your sister is a gourmet cook. Tell her you're only eating raw vegetables the next time you go to her house for dinner.

She likes *Masterpiece Theater*. You like *Desperate Housewives*. Tell her she's out of touch with the rest of the country.

You're a shopaholic. Your sister
thinks shopping is a big
waste of time. Convert her.

Your sister gives perfect dinner
parties for twelve. You can barely
grill hamburgers for six. Tell her no
one gives dinner parties anymore.

Her car asks you what
temperature you prefer when
you sit in the passenger seat.
Your car doesn't even beep
when you leave the lights on.
Say, "I understand it costs $250
to replace your windshield wipers."

She always says, "Daddy loved me best because
I was good in math." Tell her, "He always said
it was a good thing you were good in math
and could be an accountant because you were
too plain to get married."

Your sister is so easygoing she makes the Dalai Lama look tense. Ask her what she's on.

Your sister went to India and studied meditation with a maharishi. Whenever she gets angry about anything, tell her to go sit on her pillow and chant her mantra.

Her hair is silky, blond, and straight.
Yours frizzes up when there's a little dew on
the lawn. Tell her curly hair is back in style.

Convince your little sister that you're a martian and have eyes in the back of your head so you can see what she's doing when your back is to her.

Your sister can play Beethoven sonatas on the piano. You can barely manage "Chopsticks." Stuff your socks inside the piano to deaden the sound when she plays.

If your family has an embarrassing video of your older sister in diapers when she was little, be sure to show it when her boyfriend comes over.

Play hide-and-seek with your little sister and forget to find her.

Play Simon Says with your little sister and whenever she says, "May I?" always say "No."

Send her a birthday card that says on the outside, "No matter how old you get . . ." and on the inside says, "I'll always be younger!"

Tell your children your sister is deaf so they will shout in her ear when they talk to her.

Sob loudly throughout your sister's wedding.

You and your sister are painting the porch furniture. Make it more interesting by alternating one brushful of paint on the chair with one on your sister.

Your sister lives in a house with a swimming pool and you live in a studio apartment in a part of the city that hasn't yet been gentrified. Tell her she doesn't live in the real world.

Your sister is a soccer mom and you're a single office temp. Tell her you love the excitement of a new place to work every week.

Your sister runs marathons and you go to yoga class five days a week—tell her you hope she doesn't get shin splints.

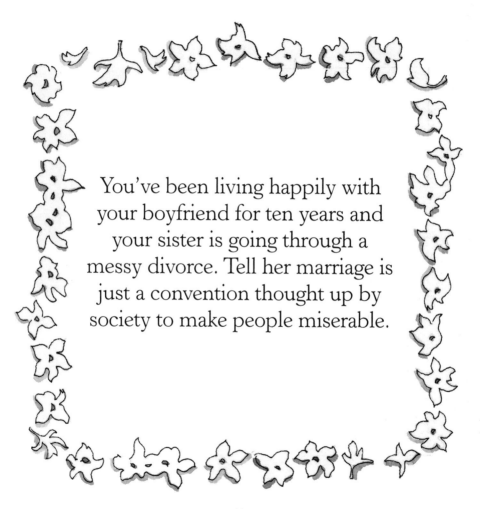

You've been living happily with your boyfriend for ten years and your sister is going through a messy divorce. Tell her marriage is just a convention thought up by society to make people miserable.

When your sister dyes her hair blond,
tell her your five favorite blonde jokes:

Why shouldn't you let a blonde
go out for a coffee break?
Because it's too hard to retrain her.

Why did eighteen blondes go to the R-rated movie?
*Because they heard that under seventeen
were not admitted.*

Did you hear about the blonde who got trapped on the escalator when the power went out?

Why did the blonde stare at the orange juice carton?
It said "Concentrate."

Why can't you tell a blonde a
knock-knock joke?
Because she gets up and answers the door.

Tell your little sister that the people on television live inside the box and come out at night and play with her toys.

Your sister was the head cheerleader and married the captain of the football team, and you smoked pot behind the gym with all the bad kids. Try not to gloat when you win your first Oscar.

It's your little sister's turn to bring the white mice home from school for the weekend. Free them from their cage, tell her you've just joined PETA, and cry, "Freedom for all living creatures!"

Your sister just got breast implants.
Tell the children they can use her as a raft in the swimming pool because she floats so well now.

You've just lost ten pounds and your sister hasn't—take her bathing suit shopping.

Your sister is nervous before her wedding. Tell her every bride is nervous about her first marriage.

You notice that your sister forgot to take the package of giblets out of the turkey at Thanksgiving before she put it in the oven. Don't tell her.

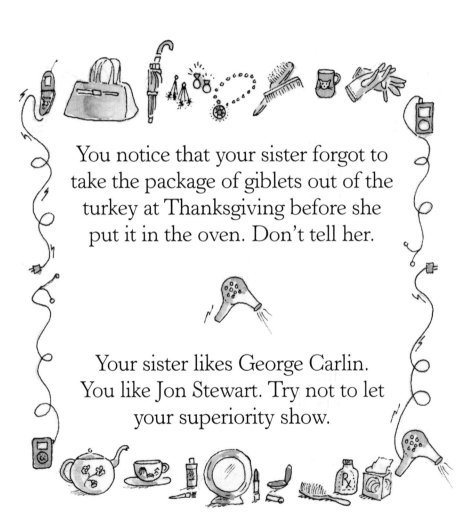

Your sister likes George Carlin. You like Jon Stewart. Try not to let your superiority show.

Tell your little sister that Santa Claus only brings toys to children who do absolutely everything their big sisters tell them to do.

When your sister is telling a funny story about her childhood, be sure to interrupt and reveal the ending of the story before she can.

Your mother is telling her friends that you
and your sister used to fight like cats and dogs,
but now that you are in your twenties you
are the best of friends. Try not to gag.

Everyone called your sister the "pretty one" when
you were children. Now she's the "cellulite queen."
Enjoy it.

Your sister is tall and the star of the high school basketball team. You're short and bad at all sports. Tell her no man wants to date a girl taller than he is.

Your sister is president of the PTA,
chairman of the board of hospital volunteers,
and runs fund-raising for her church.
You can barely keep up with the laundry.
Dedicate your first best-selling novel to her.

Tell your little sister she smells funny.

If your sister has trouble with math in school, tell her it's because your mother dropped her on her head when she was a baby and she's never been quite right ever since.

Your sister has piano legs. Tell her it's all right because no one will notice her legs—they'll be staring at her huge ears.

Tell your little sister there's a new game everyone is playing called "Hang Your Little Sister Upside Down," and if she's very good you'll let her play.

You're *American Idol.*
Your sister is *Antiques Roadshow.*
You're *Lost.* She's C-SPAN.
See that she gets help.

Your sister is a dog person.
You love cats. Tell her you've
taught your cat to use the
regular toilet in the bathroom.

Your sister's dog never jumps
on people, barks at visitors, or
chews the fringe off the rug.
Your dog flunked obedience school.
Say, "I think your dog seems a
little tense. I have the name of a
good dog psychiatrist."

Your sister plays by the rules.
You think rules were made to be broken.
Give her three margaritas and
teach her to send out for pizza.

When your sister starts losing her hearing, stand with your back to her and say all the things you always wanted to say since you were children, like "You always got your own way and I always had to do all the work."

In elementary school, you could never get the smallest toot out of a flute. Your sister played trumpet in the school band. Make her do her Louis Armstrong impression whenever you have company.

Your sister can never remember which is better—
a straight flush or a full house. Invite her over
for a friendly game of Texas Hold'em.

Set up a lemonade stand in your front yard and offer to give customers your little sister as a bonus.

Put on murder mysteries for the neighborhood kids and always make your sister play the part of the dead body.

Take your little sister trick-or-treating on Halloween and tell people she's not allowed to have candy, only apples, so you can have her share.

Everything your sister tries on in the store looks great on her. Everything you try on makes you look fat. Age will solve this problem.

Say something out of the corner of your mouth to make your sister laugh during the most serious part of the church service—then glare at her when she giggles.

Your sister's garden wins prizes every year. You can't
even keep daisies alive. Buy some rocks and pebbles
and tell her Japanese gardens are in this year.

Your sister's husband works out at the gym every day. Yours sits on the couch, watches football, and drinks beer. Tell her you've noticed how gay guys really stay in shape.

You have a nose like Barbra Streisand's. Your sister has a cute little turned-up nose like Jessica Simpson. Tell everybody she has had a nose job.

After your sister has her third face-lift, tell her every joke you can think of to bring back the laugh lines.

Tell your little sister that sex is really horrible and that's why Mommy and Daddy only did it twice.

Teach your younger sister to drive and tell her the law requires her to drive ten miles under the speed limit until she's twenty-five.

Tell your sister you gave money to a homeless drunk instead of buying her a Christmas present because you knew that's what she would want.

Give every telemarketer who calls you at dinnertime your sister's phone number because "I know she would really be interested."

Tell your sister she'll never be as old as she looks.

Start buying your sister flannel bathrobes and
L.L. Bean slippers from her fiftieth birthday on.

When your perfectly healthy sister turns sixty, give her a MedicAlert bracelet "just in case."

When your workaholic sister finally takes a weekend off, tell her, "Idle hands are the devil's workshop."

Tell your little sister she has such curly hair and dark eyes because gypsies left her on your doorstep when she was a baby.

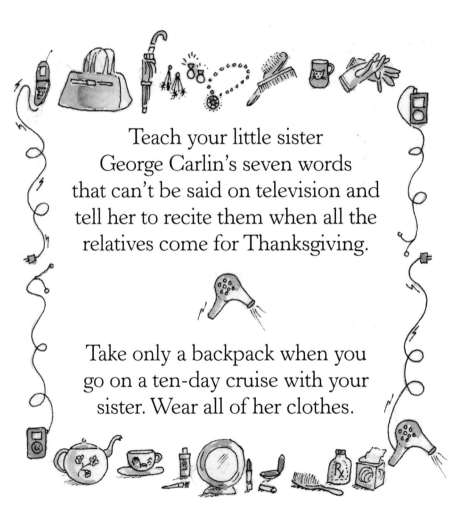

Teach your little sister
George Carlin's seven words
that can't be said on television and
tell her to recite them when all the
relatives come for Thanksgiving.

Take only a backpack when you
go on a ten-day cruise with your
sister. Wear all of her clothes.

Give your sister a large box of Godiva chocolates when she is on the Jenny Craig diet. Tell her it's a reward for losing so much weight.

When your little sister is going through her "Harriet the Spy" phase, write notes in your diary about your vow to kill her if she ever comes in your room again.

At the party for your sister's engagement
to an investment banker, show up on a
motorcycle with a vividly tattooed biker.

Take one shoe from every pair she owns
and hide them in the trunk of the car.

When your sister is suffering through
postpartum depression, tell her Tom Cruise
says there's no such thing.

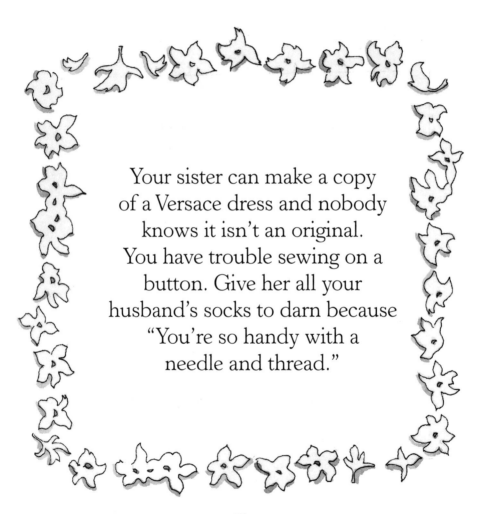

Your sister can make a copy
of a Versace dress and nobody
knows it isn't an original.
You have trouble sewing on a
button. Give her all your
husband's socks to darn because
"You're so handy with a
needle and thread."

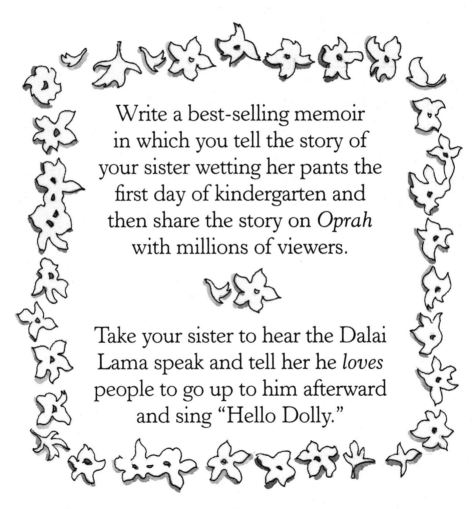

Write a best-selling memoir
in which you tell the story of
your sister wetting her pants the
first day of kindergarten and
then share the story on *Oprah*
with millions of viewers.

Take your sister to hear the Dalai
Lama speak and tell her he *loves*
people to go up to him afterward
and sing "Hello Dolly."

Remember: You're never too old to make your sister miserable. You know all the right buttons to push.

Sisters share a bond no one else has—the desire to kill each other.

There's a song from an old Rosemary Clooney musical that goes: "Lord help the mister who comes between me and my sister. And lord help the sister who comes between me and my man." Sing it to her often.

Teachers in high school expect you to have the same high grades, be president of the student council, and be the star of the soccer team just like your older sister did. Change your last name.

If your sister sleeps on your couch while
she's looking for a job after graduating from college,
don't let her eat potato chips in bed.

Give your uptight sister a satellite radio for her birthday so "you can listen to Howard Stern."

When your Republican sister invites you to a dinner party with all her conservative friends, liven up the party by bringing up the war in Iraq and how much you love the TV show *Queer Eye for the Straight Guy.*

Tell your cookie-baking, ultraconservative
sister you plan to work for the election of
Hillary Clinton for president in 2008.

When your sister has collagen injected into
her lips so she'll look like Angelina Jolie,
ask her who punched her in the mouth.

When your sister tells you her husband
wears a shower cap when he takes a bath, say,
"Isn't that a little gay?"

Your sister is slavishly following the South Beach diet. Give her a huge serving of mashed potatoes when she comes over for dinner.

Your sister is getting a little hard of hearing. Drive her crazy by moving your lips as if you are talking.

Your sister is a high-powered, successful litigator with a top law firm. Ask her if she could take a little time off to handle your house closing.

Ask your sister if she doesn't get bored saying the same lines over and over again after she just won a Tony on Broadway.

When your sister takes up painting seriously as a hobby, tell her you think her pictures are cute.

You're the ditzy Cameron Diaz sister in the movie *In Her Shoes.* Your sister is the sensible, responsible Toni Collette. Rent a grandmother like Shirley MacLaine to reconcile your differences.

When your sister hyphenates her name after she gets married, ask her how that whole long name will fit on her driver's license.

On your sister's thirtieth birthday, sign her up
for an online matchmaking service.

On her fortieth birthday, say, "You know,
you look more like Mom every year."

On her fiftieth birthday, give her a copy of
Mary McHugh's book *How Not to Become
a Little Old Lady.*

On her sixtieth birthday, remind her to sign a living will and carry an organ donor's card in her wallet.

On her seventieth birthday, send her a picture of herself at twenty with a note saying, "What happened?"

On her eightieth birthday, ask her if she wants a burial plot next to Mom and Dad's.

On her ninetieth birthday, don't bother to send a card or a present. She won't remember it's her birthday.

Be sure to tell Willard Scott about her one hundredth birthday so he can embarrass her in front of millions of people.

When your sister is pregnant with her first child, tell her God doesn't give us anything we can't stand—except labor pains.

When your sister names her first child Apocalypse Now, take the baby home and raise it yourself.

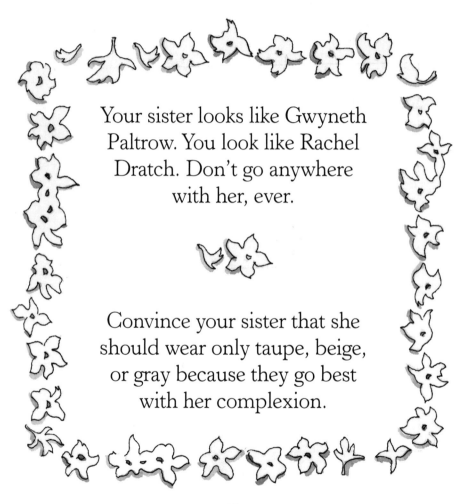

Your sister looks like Gwyneth
Paltrow. You look like Rachel
Dratch. Don't go anywhere
with her, ever.

Convince your sister that she
should wear only taupe, beige,
or gray because they go best
with her complexion.

When you babysit your little sister, let her watch really scary movies so she'll have nightmares.

Start a blog that is exclusively devoted to your sister's faults, idiosyncrasies, and inappropriate boyfriends.

When your sister has morning sickness with her first baby, tell her not to worry, you only threw up for the first six months.

At your sister's graduation from nursing school, tell everyone about the time she mixed up a patient's urinal with his water pitcher.

Your sister hates to fly. Encourage her to go on *The Amazing Race*.

Your sister is going out with a guy who could be on *The Sopranos*. Give her a bulletproof vest for her birthday.

Your sister has joined a cult and isn't allowed to speak to you anymore. Revel in it.

Program your cell phone with a special ring for your sister so when she calls to complain about something you've just done to her, you don't have to answer.

Your sister has a BlackBerry. You don't even have call waiting. Tell her you've joined the Amish.

If your sister is a member of Mensa and you can't multiply six times thirty-three in your head, tell her "ignorance is bliss" and smile a lot.

There are six sisters in your family and you're the youngest. Some day you'll be really glad.

Your sister is such a goody-goody everybody calls her Saint Anne. Make it your life's work to get her to cut loose and enjoy herself at least once.

When your sister threatens to run away
from home, help her pack.

Your sister's psychiatrist tells her that you
are the major cause of her neuroses. Tell her
you're just getting started.

Take fertility pills, have quintuplets, and tell your sister you are leaving the children to her if anything happens to you and your husband.

Make out a living will and specify that anyone else in the world is authorized to pull the plug on your ventilator except your sister.

When your little sister has her first Communion, tell her the red wine is going to stain her teeth deep purple forever.

At your sister's bat mitzvah, sneak a Pez dispenser onto the Torah ahead of time so she will giggle all through the ceremony.

When your sister starts going through menopause,
give her a little hat with a battery-operated fan on it
"for those annoying hot flashes."

You and your older sister decided to live together when you reached your eighties and she's still bossy. Pretend you can't hear a word she says and do what you want.

The best way to stop arguing with your sister is to just stop talking.

Your sister makes you feel like a dull, boring house-wife whenever she blows into town. Ask her if she'll watch the kids while you meet your lover at a motel.

Your sister is a top fashion model. You spend your life in sweat suits. The next time she comes to visit serve chocolate fudge cake, strawberry cheesecake, and spaghetti carbonara. Try not to smile when she can't eat any of it.

Think of fighting with your sister as training for life when you grow up.

When people tell you you're just like your sister, thank them and be glad they didn't say you're like your mother.

Your sister calls and tells you she is in
Moscow interviewing Vladimir Putin. You're
potty training your two-year-old. Drink several
strong margaritas while you talk to her.

You and your sister bore each other senseless.
Make a pact to see each other at the theater
or a concert where neither of you has to talk
except to say "How are you doing?"

Tell your parents they'd better keep a lawyer on retainer for your mixed-up middle sister.

When your teenage older sister leaves
her instant messaging screen open on her computer,
sneak in her room and send lewd messages
to the boys in her class.

Substitute mayonnaise for the shampoo
in her bathroom.

Your sister drives a gas-guzzling SUV.
You've just bought a hybrid, ecologically sound car.
Smile cruelly while she fills up her tank
with gas at over $3.00 a gallon.

Your sister shows up with a raggedy haircut she's just paid $150 for. Ask, "Why does your hairdresser hate you?"

Your sister just had her teeth bleached and they are so white they glow in the dark. Ask her if she can come over during the next power outage so you can cook by her mouth.

Go on *Jeopardy!* and win $17,000 in revenge for all the Cs you got in high school while you're sister was getting As.

Your sister will only buy clothes made with natural fibers, like cotton and silk, that need to be ironed or dry-cleaned. You're the permanent press queen. Use all that extra time to take a play-writing course.

Your sister loved summer camp and couldn't wait to get to the Maine woods to be uncomfortable. Remind her how much she loved roughing it every time she complains about a broken fingernail.

How old do you have to be not to be jealous of your sister anymore? Try 104—and even then. . . .

Take your golden retriever to your sister's perfect house when he's shedding.

Remind your fifty-five-year-old sister that the Age of Aquarius is long gone and that she should consider cutting her shoulder-length gray hair and wearing a little makeup now.

Invent a bad back when your sister asks you to help her move.

If you're going to steal your sister's best blouse, wear something else over it until you get to school so she'll never find out you spilled something on it.

When your little sister gets chicken pox, tell her the spots never go away.

After your sister leaves the house
for good, send her bed to Goodwill,
so she can never sleep in your
room again.

Your sister joined the Church
of Scientology because she loves
Tom Cruise and John Travolta.
Tell her about the wonderful new
psychiatrist you just found.

When your sister finally decides to get a nose job in her fifties, remind her that noses grow longer as people get older, so she'll just have to do it again in her eighties.

Unfortunately, you can't divorce
your sister when she gets really annoying.
But you can move three thousand miles
away and not give her your new
cell phone number.

Your entire dysfunctional family, including your three weird sisters, is planning a huge reunion. Say you've decided to run for president and you have to campaign in New Hampshire that weekend.

Whenever she sees you, your older sister reverts to her "I know everything and you know nothing" attitude. Be really grown up and say, as you did as a kid, "You're not the boss of me." It won't work now either.

Your sister is eighty, you're seventy-eight,
and she still asks you if you have to go to the
bathroom before you leave the house. Only now,
you're *glad* she reminds you.

You and your sister meet after work for a drink.
She gets silly on one drink and it takes three drinks
before you feel a thing. Split the tab evenly.

You and your sister go skiing together. You are on the slopes right after breakfast. She's more après-ski. Use her to find the cute guys while you're skiing.

You have never had a clue about making or managing money. Your sister is vice president of a bank. For once, listen to her advice.

Your sister moves with the grace and fluidity of a ballet dancer. You bump into chairs. Just hold onto the thought that she'll get old some day and bump into chairs, too.

Your sister is an accountant who loves to talk about her work. Practice not falling asleep when you're with her.

Your sister drives like a maniac. Never sit up front in the passenger seat. Sit in the back and keep your eyes closed until you get to your destination.

When your younger sister graduates magna cum laude from an Ivy League college, just hug your new baby and love your life.

Your sister comes for the weekend and complains about your cooking, your housekeeping, your children, and your husband. Wear earplugs and smile. Wait at least a year before you invite her again.

Put a positive spin on your sister's constant nagging and pushing you to be a better person and stop lying around the house listening to music and talking on the phone. You left home to get away from her and it was the best thing you ever did.

Your sister gives you the same thing for Christmas every year—bed socks she knitted herself. Tell her you always sleep in the nude but the socks make a nice soft bed for your puppy.

When you send your holiday
letter with your Christmas cards,
say that your goody-goody
sister is in jail for selling marijuana
but that you hope she'll be home
for New Year's Eve.

Your sister recycles *everything*.
Ask her if there's a way you
can recycle her into a sister
who is more fun.

When your sister turns up
with three new tattoos, ask her
if your child can bring her into
school for show-and-tell.

Your sister has just married a man with three
teenaged children. Try not to laugh.

You think your older brother is God.
Your sister thinks he is typically male and a pig.
Your brother brought the perfect man home and
you married him. Your sister is still single.

When your sister monopolizes the phone
every day after school, steal her cell phone and
make all your calls on that.

Go into a chat room online called
"Really Hot Girls and How to Find Them,"
and give them your sister's e-mail.

When your little sister asks you where babies
come from, tell her they grow from watermelon
seeds just after she has swallowed some.

Or you could say that when a boy kisses you,
you will automatically have a baby
nine months afterward.

Before your sister has her first mammogram, reassure her that it's not so bad—sort of like having a garage door come down on your breast.

Your sister volunteers to be a Big Sister to a disadvantaged child. Tell her you wish she'd be half as nice to you, her real sister.

You discover that your perfect housewife sister is growing pot in her herb garden. Smoke some together and really bond with her before you turn her in.

Resist the temptation to go to the same college as your twin sister. Even the Olsen twins couldn't make *that* work.

Your sister is a klutz and has decided to join the police force. Try to discourage her so the crime rate won't go way up in your town.

Tell your sister that see-through blouses aren't really for women with A cups.

Your sister still wears the white boots she bought when Nancy Sinatra's "These Boots Were Made for Walkin'" came out in the '70s. Some day when she's out, give them to the Salvation Army.

Your sister's favorite movie is *Sleepless in Seattle*. Tell her to stop going to the top of the Empire State Building—Tom Hanks isn't up there.

Tell your little sister that she shouldn't worry about the bear that lives in her bedroom closet because he only comes out when he's *really* hungry.

Your sister won every
Girl Scout badge they had.
You had trouble growing a plant
out of an avocado seed for the
gardening badge. Thirty years later,
nobody really cares about
either of those things.

The next time your sister criticizes you for not spending enough time with your children because of your career, tell her you know for a fact that her teenagers wish she would spend more time out of the house.

Your sister never returns calls made to
her home phone because she communicates
only by cell phone. Call her on her cell and use up
her minutes with long, boring stories about your
children and their teachers.

While you were growing up, your sister was
the "quiet, deep one" and you were the talkative,
superficial one. Don't invite her to appear on
your Emmy-winning TV talk show.

Your sister just lost six pounds eating healthily on Weight Watchers. Tell her you lost twelve pounds on your own chocolate and wine diet.

Your sister has a perfect fashion sense and always looks pulled together. Tell her your new nickname for her is "Miss Superficiality."

Now that she's twenty-one, your sister has decided to dress only in black. Ask her whose funeral she's going to.

Your sister was voted "Most Likely to Be a CEO" in high school. You were voted "Most Likely to Marry a Rock Star." Now you're running a Fortune 500 company and she's a Bon Jovi groupie. Go figure.

Tell everyone on the school bus that your sister gets carsick so nobody will sit next to her.

Tell your little sister she's just going to *love* camp— that there are hardly any snakes and most of them aren't poisonous.

When your sister eats in a restaurant and spills spaghetti sauce on her white blouse as usual, tell her she should always order food the same color as the clothes she is wearing.

When your sister calls you at the office for the tenth time in one day to tell you the latest cute thing her new baby did, put her on hold.